HOW **MUSIC**
CAN MAKE
YOU **BETTER**

HOW **MUSIC** CAN MAKE YOU **BETTER**

INDRE VISKONTAS, PhD

CHRONICLE BOOKS
SAN FRANCISCO

Library of Congress Cataloging-in-Publication Data available.

ISBN: 978-1-4521-7192-0

Manufactured in China.

Design by Vanessa Dina

10 9 8 7 6 5 4 3 2 1

Chronicle Books LLC
680 Second Street
San Francisco, California 94107
www.chroniclebooks.com

Chronicle books and gifts are available at special quantity discounts to
corporations, professional associations, literacy programs, and other
organizations. For details and discount information, please contact our
premiums department at corporatesales@chroniclebooks.com or at
1-800-759-0190.

MUSIC
IS
POWERFUL

When I tell people I'm an opera singer, they are surprised to meet a modern-day unicorn: mysterious, rare, and, let's face it, pretty archaic. Who in their right mind would devote all that time to training an operatic voice when the art form is irrelevant for most people? I can understand this reaction.

But it breaks my heart when the now duly impressed person tells me that they love music but know nothing about it. They ask if their favorite singer—Adele, Bono, Bob Dylan—has a good voice. They seem ashamed of their musical taste, doubting that the music they enjoy is objectively great. Music has become caged in a caste system where even the most passionate admirers question their ability to distinguish nobility from commoners. And the performance of music has been ripped from the clutches of amateurs and reserved for the privileged class of "professionals."

How did we get here? Music has always been for the masses. Even opera, whose first audiences played cards, smoked, drank, and conversed loudly throughout the show, challenged the singers to capture their attention with emotion and vocal acrobatics. These humble beginnings are a far cry from the elitist reputation opera now enjoys. Today, many people avoid it altogether, embarrassed because they just don't find the music moving.

Why do I find opera sublime while others find it boring? As both a singer and a cognitive neuroscientist, I like to combine art and science to help answer this and other questions.

Many of us think music exists in the ether—while it defies definition, we know it when we hear it. But the truth is that *we only hear it when we know it*. Music isn't music until our minds make it so. Sound can be noise in one context but music in another.

Like many aspects of our personalities, we can thank our parents and our raging teenage hormones for much of our musical tastes. Two forces that shape those tastes are early exposure, when we first develop a relationship with sound, and the roller-coaster emotional ride of adolescence.

But no matter where you came from and where that ride ultimately took you, music has almost certainly left its indelible mark. Whether you have perfect pitch or can't hold a tune, whether you have B-sides that you can't let go of or guilty pleasure music reserved for road trips, music has shaped your mind. And neuroscience can show you how.

Humans are bizarre creatures: We value many things that don't ensure our survival or propagate our genes. Perhaps then it's not so surprising that we spend our money and time listening to and creating meaningful sounds. But for curious extraterrestrial visitors, our love affair with meaningful sound would be baffling.

Music is essential to so many of our activities: watching movies, shopping, working out, eating out, cheering on sports teams, commuting to work. Music has the power to connect people, to change brains, to incite violence and tame beasts, to give us energy or heal our pain. But it's our minds that turn noise into this panacea.

Each way of consuming or creating music has a unique neural signature and leads to a unique subjective experience. Music affects us in so many different ways that, when they are all taken together, few brain regions are left untouched. That's why music can be a lifeline in the face of devastating brain conditions, be it Alzheimer's disease or a traumatic brain injury.

In this guide, we'll first find out what music actually is and how it works. Then we'll explore how it can help or heal our minds and bodies. Finally, we'll turn to how music can change society. This book will show you just how ethereal and magical music is, that there is no one right way to listen or play, and that extracting meaning from sound is one of the greatest gifts that natural selection has given us.

PART I

HOW DO OUR BRAINS TURN SOUND INTO MUSIC?

"You can't touch music—it exists only at the moment it is being apprehended— and yet it can profoundly alter how we view the world and our place in it."

—DAVID BYRNE,
HOW MUSIC WORKS

Music isn't in sound waves. It's not in your ears. It's not on the page.

It's in your brain.

Sound can be noise in one context and music in another. The difference? How you listen and how your brain interprets the signal: Is it random noise, or is there a meaningful pattern?

Just by repeating a spoken phrase over and over, you can turn it into song. Try it. Or check out Diana Deutsch's Speech-to-Song Illusion (http://deutsch. ucsd.edu/) in which the spoken phrase "sometimes behave so strangely" turns into music right before your ears.

Repetition is the one feature of music that is almost universal, ubiquitous across cultures and genres, except in twentieth-century art music ("contemporary classical"), which explicitly avoids it. Which is why this "new music" can be very hard to listen to and why, when an orchestra programs too much of it in a season, they quickly hear complaints from their donors.

Why repetition? Because our brains are tuned to detect change, not constancy. When something repeats, we ignore it. But if it's slightly varied, we keep listening because we detect something worth processing. We begin to find new meaning embedded in the sound itself. Repetition gives noise a recognizable structure. Variations in repetition create meaning. And sound + structure + meaning = music. Voilà!

Pattern repetition is how we learn the grammar of music, and that structure distinguishes music from random noise. Some structural elements are common across many types of music, like a move from dissonance (tension) to consonance (release). Others define specific genres, like the repeating bassline groove in most pop songs. But most pieces don't settle for pure repetition. They include variations on themes, which keep our interest and reveal ever deeper layers of truth.

Equally important in the definition of music is the context in which we hear sound. Ever wonder why audiophiles spend more time and money setting up their home stereo than their bedroom? *Where* we hear music can influence how our brains respond to it.

In the concert hall, we sit still and listen carefully. On the subway platform, we pretend to ignore a busking musician, burying our heads in our phones. At the gym, we fill our ears with beats, tuning out the noise of elliptical machines and grunting weight lifters.

Even silence, in the right context, can be profoundly musical. The eminent experimental composer John Cage wrote a piece called *4′33″* which can be "played" on any combination of instruments. All the performers need to do is *not* play their instruments for the duration of the piece. The music is in the sounds that the listeners hear while the players are not playing. John Cage considered it his most important work.

So if a tree falls in the forest and there is no one there to hear it, it doesn't make a sound. Because sound is created by brains. Sure, the falling tree triggers compressions and rarefactions in the air, but those don't become *sound* until our inner ears transduce that signal into the language of the brain. Until then, they are just moving molecules of air.

Silence can be music in the right context, but without a listener to interpret the noise, even the greatest symphony isn't music.

Now you might not agree that *4´33″* is actually music. Maybe your definition is more specific, including organized sound and the communication of an idea or emotion. And you'd be totally right, since it's your own brain that's creating and recognizing the music as such. Something special happens when our brains decide that what we're hearing is musical.

That special something is still mysterious, but it likely has to do with the structure we recognize once we're familiar with a certain type of music. We learn structure explicitly by studying music theory, or implicitly by listening. You don't have to go to music school to get it.

"Country music is three chords and the truth," said songwriter Harlan Howard in a *Rolling Stone* interview. Howard's definition applies to just about any popular music yet leaves room for that *je ne sais quoi* that defines a genre and for the ideas that a specific piece communicates.

Howard also reminds us that structure isn't enough to make music musical. Music also requires "the truth." I once did a little experiment with a chamber music ensemble to highlight this idea. We played a piece strictly according to what was written on the page. When told to speed up, we did so metronomically. When told to play louder or softer, we did, again, with no true intention. It was a technically good performance, but there was no music made. We all felt a little icky afterward.

Musicality reveals a deep, dark secret of humanity: We are flawed creatures. When a performance is too perfect, it's less human.

Ayanna Howard, an engineer who builds artificially intelligent robots, told me that when a robot is too perfect, people don't trust it. One team was engineering a robot to lead people out of a burning hospital. The robot would use real-time information from the fire alarm system to know which corridors to use and which to avoid. But the first prototype had a flaw: The humans didn't trust it.

So the engineers coded in a few errors—the robot would start in one direction, stop as if realizing it had made a mistake, apologize, and then take the correct route—people were much more likely to trust it, since making mistakes is a very human thing to do!

If musicians don't push and pull at the tempo, vary the dynamics, or give us another sign that what they are expressing is human and intentional, we can't relate to them and we don't find the music, well, musical.

Music's underlying structure isn't strict. Instead, there are statistical regularities—probabilities of where the beats will fall, for example. We learn these probabilities without even knowing it, and they set up our expectations for what sounds will come next.

Then musicians build on those expectations, feeding us what we want and surprising us at the same time. Music we love rides this fine line between familiarity and novelty. Many jazz musicians, for example, delay the first beat in a bar and then accelerate to catch up. It's what gives jazz its cool factor—and makes it feel very human. We even say that the performance has "soul."

But music is a representation of life, not life itself. We're generally aware that we're listening to something that was created to give us an experience, rather than having an emotional reaction to something that actually happened to us. While music can elicit deep and authentic emotions, the musicians themselves don't need to feel all those emotions in the moment. They just need to make the audience believe that they're real.

It took me a long time as a performer to understand this. When I was a teenager participating in a singing competition, I received a piece of criticism I'll never forget. The judges said that I wasn't musical. I was deeply hurt because I had chosen pieces that I truly loved and understood. But somehow I had failed to show this to the judges.

I put that memory away for a long time and worked on my technique. Then I was cast as Beth in Mark Adamo's opera *Little Women*. If you remember Louisa May Alcott's book, you know Beth is the sister who dies. In the opera, she expires after a series of floating, quiet, high notes.

In rehearsals, I found the aria so moving that I couldn't get through it without breaking down. But crying is not good when you're trying to float a bunch of high notes. So I had to keep my emotions in check while remaining in character and making the music expressive.

I realized that by the time I'm in front of an audience, it doesn't matter anymore whether *I* feel my character's feelings. It only matters that the audience believes that *my character* is feeling those feelings.

That's true of any music: By coming into the concert hall, the opera house, the bar, or any other venue, the audience tacitly signs an agreement. They do not expect a real rendering of an event. Who, after all, would choose to lose someone they love, or feel pain or desperation (the most common themes of pop songs) in public? But by listening to music, we can simultaneously contemplate the ideas or feel the feelings, while having a conversation about how the idea or feeling is being expressed. We know it's fake to some degree, but we can appreciate how the musicians are communicating it.

In the midst of a breakup or some other loss, I can listen to Tracy Chapman's "Give Me One Reason" and enjoy not only the emotional catharsis, but also the brilliant way she's captured a universal experience. I can nod along and say, yeah, that's *exactly* what it's like. And then I feel a bit better and less alone. Listening to music lets us work through our emotions in a safe environment and walk away if the feelings get too intense. It provides a lens through which we can examine our lives.

We are driven by the search for meaning. And ultimately music is meaningful sound that transcends speech. Whereas speech can be more specific—I can play the violin until I'm blue in the face but you still won't bring home a carton of milk—music's power is in the multiple ways we interpret it. Our brains are primed to search for meaning in chaos. We look for patterns and feel rewarded when we find them, even if they aren't real—the sleeping giant in the mountainside, the man in the moon. And music is a treasure trove of hidden jewels.

Anyone who spends precious mental energy trying to solve a puzzle, *for fun*, understands the pleasure of discovering meaning. If an alien civilization might be baffled by our obsession with structured sound, just imagine how they would react to crossword puzzles or, worse still, a punning competition.

Yet finding multiple hidden meanings is pleasurable. Scientists Irving Biederman and Ed Vessel point out that we have more opioid receptors in parts of our cortex (where associations are made) compared with our primary sensory regions (where stimuli are initially processed). You need only to hear the term *opioid epidemic* to remind yourself that neurochemicals binding to opioid receptors make us feel good—drugs that mimic our brain's own opioids are highly addictive. So activating more such receptors can give you greater pleasure.

For example, when you first look at a painting, your primary visual cortex notices edges and colors, but opioid receptors in this brain region are few and far between. Then, as the information travels farther into the brain, and the edges and colors turn into objects, more opioid receptors are activated. Finally, in the parts of the brain where those objects are associated with memories, identity, emotions, or culture, the density of opioid receptors is greater still.

But once you've made those associations, the experience becomes ingrained in your brain, and you don't get the same rush. It's the neural equivalent of "been there, done that," as Biederman says. So we seek out novel experiences that are rich in interpretative potential: We are infovores.

Sometimes I listen to music in the background, just to keep my energy up. But my most profound experiences come when I'm paying close attention, searching and finding those hidden jewels. And when those discoveries help me understand an experience, like losing my dad, or meeting my son for the first time, in ways that mere words fall short of, I feel a kind of euphoria that defines, for me, what it means to be alive.

We get bored when music is too simple. If it's too repetitive, we tune out, just as we tune out the feeling of the clothes on our bodies or the sounds that our homes make at night.

When you're three and just learning about musical structure, "The Wheels on the Bus" can be very compelling. When you're thirty, it's torture. Because there's nothing new to discover.

On the other end of the spectrum, music that's too complex can be just as irritating. If you've ever been forced to sit through a live performance that is incomprehensible to you—maybe a minimalist opera by Philip Glass, or free improvisation by jazz musicians— you know how boring music can be. I'll never forget an interminable evening I spent at a jazz club in Manhattan, before I knew what to listen for.

A lot of people are turned off by complex music like opera and other classical music because not only do they find it boring, but they also feel they *should* like it, since it's considered "high art." Classical music used to be much more common in our daily lives. On the radio, in department stores, at the dentist's office. But you can grow up today and never be exposed to it.

Without that exposure, you don't learn where and how to find the meaning.

We are bored by music that's too simple and too complex—the most enjoyable music is just right. But what does that mean? And why is that the case? Music is enjoyable in part because we can follow along, find meaning in the sound, and still be surprised. Like a good story, good music sets up certain events and then keeps us hooked by delaying them or taking us in unexpected (but still plausible) directions.

Children love songs with predictable hooks. But as we learn the structure of music, we need less predictability and more complexity to stay engaged. A new genre makes us regress to childhood, as we need to understand the structure before we can engage with it. A novice jazz listener will prefer a riff that's repeated until she starts to learn the language of jazz. With experience, she'll be able to pick up ever more complicated riffs and follow along with an expert improviser. That's what I learned when I studied jazz. Now the performance that once bored me to tears would be a riveting emotional journey.

The more we listen to and learn about a genre, the more we can appreciate its best performers and innovators. So if you don't "get" a particular genre, the cure is to listen to it more, not less; 50,000,000 Elvis fans can't be wrong, after all.

That's why I can't get enough of the second act finale of Wolfgang Amadeus Mozart's *The Marriage of Figaro*: It's so complex that I discover something new every time I sing or listen to it. Mozart was a master of infinite variation on a pattern. Each variation is meaningful, often revealing something profound.

Once a complex piece is familiar, we can continue to discover new meanings without having to start from scratch processing the superficial details. The memory trace of that superficial perceptual processing is already ingrained in our brains.

If I don't have the mental energy to listen carefully to new music, it's hard for me to enjoy it. But a well-loved album gives me both pleasure and energy. It's like watching a complicated movie for the first time: You spend mental fuel figuring out what's happening and predicting what will happen, and evaluating whether it's any good. But once you know the ending, and that you liked it, you can enjoy it again without all that work. We often avoid spoilers. But science has shown that even when a story is spoiled, we report it as just as enjoyable (if not more so) as when we don't know the ending. That's because we remember the gist but not the details that make a great story compelling.

But it's important to pair repeated listens with a bit of research about the cultural context of the music. That's just as true for Mozart as it is for Tupac.

Some people hate a particular genre. I've done surveys of musical preferences, and it's not just opera: Genres like heavy metal and hip-hop seem to draw their fair share of haters too. The screaming and chaotic noise of heavy metal grates on some, while others object to the aggressive lyrics and subversive messages of hip-hop. But Mozart wasn't exactly kind to women or respectful of authority, either.

I learned a lot about hip-hop from the Gimlet media podcast *Mogul*, which traces the origins and development of the genre. By using two turntables at the same time, DJs could extend the percussive breaks in a piece of music and allow the dancing to continue uninterrupted.

Understanding that the turntable technique emerged during block parties in low-income neighborhoods in 1970s New York gave me a better appreciation of how a group of people found an innovative way to temporarily escape a difficult existence.

In addition to vastly improving spontaneous dance parties, hip-hop provided disenfranchised youth with a voice. Rhythmic wordplay, insults, and boasting speech over a beat gave birth to rapping.

So listening for seamless beat-matching and clever political and social commentary helps me find the nuggets of meaning that my brain enjoys in hip-hop. Which helps me understand the experiences of hip-hop artists, feel empathy for the performers, and recognize a part of myself in their observations.

Even when I'm evaluating music in a genre I've studied for decades, I still reserve judgment until I've taken the time to understand what the composer is trying to say. I often sing recently composed contemporary classical music that hasn't been performed often or even at all. I can't just glance at the score or listen to a MIDI file to know whether I want to invest the time to learn it.

I need to listen to or play it multiple times before I can pass judgment.

One reason is that new music often takes time and effort to understand. But there's another, simpler reason. As I mentioned in the last chapter, familiarity breeds preference. Psychologists call this phenomenon the "mere exposure effect." Simply hearing a new piece a second time makes people report that they like it more. So if a new piece doesn't move me at first, is it simply a matter of learning the patterns, or is it just not that good?

Even baby chickens show the mere exposure effect. Scientist Robert Zajonc had a graduate student expose fertile chicken eggs to one of two tones. Once the chicks hatched, they preferred the tone that had been played while they were still in their eggs to the new tone.

But not all music is easy to like after a few listens. In the 1960s, Henry Cross, Charles Halcomb, and William Matter exposed two groups of rats to twelve hours of music every day for the first 52 days of their lives. One group heard Mozart, the other Arnold Schoenberg. Then they got to take a break from music for 15 days. Finally, it was time to test their preferences.

Each rat was put into a chamber with two sides: Previously unheard Mozart music played on one side and new Schoenberg music on the other. Rats exposed to Mozart in the first phase of the experiment chose to spend most of their time on the Mozart side. But control animals and the Schoenberg group showed no preference. Even rats can recognize the enduring genius of Mozart, but it takes specially trained human brains to "get" Schoenberg. It's not surprising, then, that virtually every Western-raised child can sing a little Mozart (the "Alphabet Song," or "Twinkle, Twinkle Little Star") but few of them walk to school humming "Pierrot Lunaire."

But we can't say that tonal, melody-rich Mozartian music is innately more appealing (or less aversive) than atonal Schoenberg. Perhaps the lowly rat can "understand" Mozart more easily than the more complex, less repetitive music of Schoenberg. We don't know that rats actually *like* it. And although many of us start our musical journey with Mozart while singing our ABCs, most of us gravitate toward other composers and genres as our musical tastes form. We find our sweet spot, just like Goldilocks did, but only after testing many bowls of porridge.

If I had to sum up what the brain does in one sentence, I would say that it predicts the future. Virtually every brain system, from perception to memory to decision making, is about predicting consequences. We look for patterns because they give us hints about what's coming next. The search for meaning can be reinterpreted as a search for patterns or for intentions in others so we can predict their behavior.

That's why stories can be so addictive: They tap into our reward system, much the same way that other goal-directed behaviors do. And music is a bit like storytelling: There's a beginning, a middle, and an end, and we enjoy figuring out what's going to happen next.

A great story builds tension. Suspense is created when the audience knows something that the characters don't—they can predict consequences that aren't obvious to the protagonist. Music, too, builds tension until an inevitable release: If there's dissonance, then (in most genres) consonance is around the corner. Even babies can recognize dissonance. When the intervals between two notes are too close, the music sounds wrong. Tense. And we want it to resolve into consonance, when the notes sound harmoniously "right," which babies and most of the rest of us prefer. We know that release is coming. At least we hope it is. The question is when. If it doesn't come, then we are dissatisfied. If it *does* arrive, we exhale because everything has turned out okay.

But the longer the musician can draw out the process, while still holding the audience's interest, the more effective the climax will be. We want to feel the music edging its way to a satisfying conclusion. The more you want something, the better it feels when you get it. And for some people, that climax can trigger a physiological reaction: the chills.

For people who get the chills, the experience is highly reproducible. Listening to certain pieces leaves them with those pleasurable goose bumps 77 percent of the times that they hear it.

And the pieces most likely to give someone the chills have some features in common. They are usually slow, more ballad than upbeat pop song. They often include a solo treble voice emerging from a cacophony of sound, like Whitney Houston's voice in "I Will Always Love You," the guitar solo in "Hotel California," or the first violins in Edward Elgar's "Nimrod" from the

Enigma Variations. And the chills happen either at the climax, after a long buildup (as in Samuel Barber's *Adagio for Strings*), or when something unexpected happens—an abrupt shift in tempo, dynamics, or texture.

We're just starting to understand the neurochemistry and brain activation patterns that underlie our experience of pleasure in music. But as artists of all kinds, or any purveyors of pleasure, have long known, rewarding experiences are made up of two parts: the anticipation phase and the consummatory phase. Wanting and liking. The building up of tension and its eventual release.

Pleasure is the death of desire. But the greater the desire, the greater the pleasure.

The neurotransmitter dopamine plays a major role during the anticipation phase, which is why I call it the "salience chemical." It signals the approach of something meaningful (good or bad). This is the wanting phase: the tense expectation of something big just around the corner.

Then, if the thing that appears is good, both dopamine and mu-opioid receptors are activated. The ultimate effect is more dopamine in our brains' pleasure centers, such as the nucleus accumbens, which makes us feel good.

Both processes come into play when we listen to music. Scientists have found that the caudate (the brain region that tracks pleasurable or painful things in our environment) is full of dopamine in the lead-up to a musical climax. And when we finally get the chills, dopamine and endogenous opioids spike in the nucleus accumbens (the part of the reward circuit that gives us intense pleasure). If you implant an electrode into a rat's nucleus accumbens and teach it to press a lever that sends a stimulating pulse to that region, it will press the lever all day long, eschewing food, water, and sex, even until it is close to death. It feels that good. At least to the rat. We haven't quite been able to replicate the result by stimulating the nucleus accumbens in humans. If we did, we'd likely stagnate as a species, choosing to do nothing but engage in this stimulation. We'd become vulnerable to an alien species, who could keep us happy in little stimulating vats and harness our energy for their own purposes.

Unfortunately for the evil aliens, we are conscious of the fact that pleasure is fleeting, and we become satiated. For most of us, happiness requires more than feeling pleasure; we also want to find meaning in a life well lived. But music taps into both of these needs. It can make us feel good and satisfy our search for meaning.

The one piece of music most likely to give someone the chills is Barber's *Adagio for Strings,* sometimes called the saddest music ever written. (Why does sad music feel good? We'll cover that a bit later.) The piece can be pared down to one long scale progression. Listening to it, we all know where it wants to go, but it takes a meandering path to its resolution.

We can all relate. Who among us hasn't struggled to get to where we want to be? When the melody finally reaches its destination, it's as though the sun has broken through the clouds—we feel pleasure at the release of tension, the return to the tonic, just as we do when we finally come home, but it's the journey that resonates with us.

What's the second most common piece to give someone the chills? A DJ's remix of Barber's piece. Go figure.

On the way to giving us the chills, great musical pieces like Beethoven's late quartets, Led Zeppelin's "Stairway to Heaven," or Adele's "Hello" slow down time, as the release of tension is delayed further and further.

But music can also accelerate time: As many students will attest, music makes study hours fly by. A disaster at SoulCycle is a broken sound system. And a patient lost to Alzheimer's disease can suddenly come alive by listening to music from his twenties. Perhaps the time machine many of us dream about is already encased in iTunes.

Great musicians harness time to highlight the emotions behind the music, to help us find multiple meanings, and to give us new experiences.

Jazz musicians, for example, will set a steady beat with drums or bass. Then the soloist will delay their downbeat and accelerate the rest of the beats in the measure to catch up. This is exactly what Chet Baker does in "My Funny Valentine." We know what's coming, since most of us could sing the tune in time on our own, but he never gives us exactly what we expect, delaying one note and speeding up another. By stretching and compressing time, he helps us feel the emotions behind the words.

By bending time, musicians also invite us to listen for multiple meanings and give us a richer experience of sound. Much like mindfulness meditation (during which a person focuses on things they often ignore, like the breath), music allows us to extract more information from the sounds we're hearing. This richer experience forms more memories, which emphasizes the illusion that time has slowed down.

One reason time speeds up as we get older is that we have fewer new experiences. When our days are driven by routine, we don't remember them as well. Exposing ourselves to new experiences can make time feel less like a speeding train and more like a leisurely Sunday ride, and music offers many novel adventures. Even a piece we've heard a hundred times, like "My Funny Valentine," feels new when musicians play with time.

Music can divide generations, and it can be hard to appreciate or even recognize sounds from a different era as music. Music is subjective, and which music is "great" is up for debate. Sure, Mozart and Ludwig van Beethoven have good reputations, but Adele and Jay-Z boast more living fans than all of classical music put together. Liking Mozart is supposed to signal sophistication, but nothing alienates an audience more than making them feel stupid. Is there such a thing as universally great music?

"I think the first and most important thing to realize is the people who created the music, whether we're talking about dead euro white males from a phallocentric empire or Jimi Hendrix, these are people just like us, these are working class and middle class people. Composers are not rich people. They might work for rich people because that's how you make a buck. But they are not rich people per se, they are people who are great artisans and craftspeople who use their ability to make music to make a living. And as a result, all music is relevant to its time; and all really good music, like any good art, becomes universal. It transcends its time and place because it has enough metaphor, enough analogue, enough pure beauty to communicate with people in any time and any place."

—COMPOSER AND HISTORIAN ROBERT GREENBERG, *CADENCE* PODCAST

How do we develop musical taste? For most, it comes down to two things: exposure and hormones. Two periods in your life shape many of your musical preferences: the highly suggestible time of early childhood, when the brain is tripling in size and trying to make sense of the world, and the teenage years, when a deluge of hormones coincides with the final wiring and a push to separate ourselves from our parents.

By age two, toddlers are already developing their sound palate, preferring the music of their own culture and learning musical structure by repeating melodies and rhythms ad nauseam. Infants raised in noisy environments learn to tune out sound, while those whose parents listen intently to music will orient toward it, recruiting larger swaths of their brains to process it.

Then come the tumultuous teen years. Our brains are feverishly wiring up, particularly in our prefrontal cortex, which isn't fully formed until our twenties. Add to that a powerful concoction of hormones that send us on wild emotional rides, ensuring that we remember the very good and the very bad as we learn to navigate the world on our own. This creates the perfect recipe for developing musical taste.

Music is a powerful tool for social bonding, and when we separate ourselves from our parents in adolescence, we sometimes gravitate toward music that they might hate but that defines our burgeoning identity. Many decades later, we can recognize that this music is not particularly "good," yet we find it immensely pleasurable.

"Ninety percent of what I'm listening to overall is like the same tape of Bob Marley's *Greatest Hits*. Like, how did I become one of those people on late-night TV where they sell anthologies to you and you buy them?"

—STANFORD PSYCHOLOGY PROFESSOR ROBERT SAPOLSKY, *RADIOLAB* PODCAST

Human behavior expert Robert Sapolsky was utterly annoyed by his twenty-one-year-old research assistant, who was very good at his job but had a terrible habit of listening to different music every day. One of the sad consequences of aging is that we stop trying new things. So our musical tastes get stuck in our twenties. Sapolsky found the constant variety annoying. Yet his research assistant's instinct to search and openness to new experiences was markedly age appropriate.

Even if we're older and more crotchety, listening to music from other genres and eras can wake us up again—though it takes a bit of work to learn what to listen for. Despite our age-earned wisdom, a new piece of music requires many listens before our brain learns its underlying structure and meaning.

Anyone can learn to appreciate music. But can everyone produce it? People often tell me they can't carry a tune, that they were born unable to sing. This mindset is a modern tragedy. Whereas music used to be performed by nearly everyone, it's becoming the exclusive domain of the professional.

Do you consider yourself tone-deaf? If so, could you tell the difference between your mother and your best friend on the phone? If you can, you're not technically deaf to tones, since it's the timbre of the voice that separates the two.

Almost all of us are born with what seems like a particular musical taste. Babies prefer the music that is most common in their culture; for Western infants, that means nice symmetrical chords rather than dissonance. When, in an otherwise consonant melody, a note is out of place, most Western listeners will notice. But a person with true tone deafness, or *amusia*, will not. People born without the ability to recognize or hum familiar tunes suffer from what we call amusia. It's very rare, only about 4 percent of the population, but it does seem to run in families. If you're reading this book, you likely don't have it. But if you never understood why no one in your family can sing a recognizable "Happy Birthday," well, maybe you're on to something.

More likely, if you think you can't sing, you just have trouble making the sound that you hear in your head. That's called pitch matching, and it's largely a matter of the right type of practice.

Practice involves more than endlessly repeating scales. There's a psychological component, since performance anxiety often results in muscle tension and dryness in the throat—which isn't conducive to singing.

Great singers aren't born that way. Even songbirds have to go through a period of learning, during which they make sounds, evaluate them, and try to do better.

In fact, there are many similarities between how songbirds compose new songs and how we're able to make a seemingly infinite variety of vocalizations. In both species, there are direct connections between the part of the brain that controls muscles and the muscles of our voice box. That's not true of our cousin species (say, chimpanzees or chickens) that haven't evolved the ability to imitate and create new sounds vocally.

Great singers, whether zebra finches or sopranos, develop connections between their brains and their vocal muscles with practice. Which means that you can too. I was by no means a natural—it took me more than a decade to build that wiring. Just imagine what you could do after that much training.

Sometimes we can't get enough of music. But other times, music can't get enough of us, and a tune gets stuck on repeat, much to our dismay. We call these stuck songs "earworms," or "involuntary musical imagery," to get scientific.

By some estimates, 98 percent of us experience earworms; and they are equally common in men and women but last longer and are more irritating for women. If you like music, you're more susceptible to earworms. And most often, earworms contain lyrics, not just instrumental melodies.

Where do they come from? And what on earth are they for? They might be related to other involuntary behaviors—and alleviated, if particularly bad, by medications used to treat obsessive-compulsive disorder (OCD). Why? We turn to our friend the caudate once again.

The caudate nucleus is part of our motivated learning circuits. It's responsible for various things, including tracking what we should approach and what we should avoid, given past experiences. It also plays an important role in learning habits.

In music, the caudate seems active during the anticipation phase of a melody that will give us the chills, as I've mentioned. But it's also important for feeling the beat, which makes sense if you know it's interconnected with our motor system (we don't hear the beat, we *feel* it in our bodies).

For a long time, scientists focused on the anxiety component of OCD, but it turns out that OCD symptoms are perhaps more tied to habit learning than to anxiety.

In people with OCD, the caudate nucleus is in overdrive when they're engaging in a habitual behavior like washing their hands. The same is true in other compulsive behaviors like binge eating or drug abuse. There's even compelling evidence that food avoidance in people with anorexia nervosa is a learned habit, reflected in a hyperactive caudate nucleus, rather than just a strong desire to be thin.

And an earworm might be just another thought that an overzealous caudate nucleus turns into a habit, like tapping along to a song without even thinking about it.

How do you stop earworms? The most effective way seems to be by using your working memory for something else—solving a crossword puzzle or playing chess. Or you can work through the musical fragment in your head to reach its climax, rather than endlessly repeating it without getting anywhere. Then be sure to go and focus on something else so the worm doesn't return.

PART 2

HOW CAN MUSIC HEAL OUR MINDS AND BODIES?

MUSIC REPAIRS BROKEN CIRCUITS

Before she was shot in the head, Gabby Giffords was a talented orator. But after a bullet decimated her left frontal cortex, she was silenced. Months of speech therapy brought painfully slow progress. Until one remarkable day.

After trying several times to pronounce the word "light," Giffords broke down in tears. Her speech therapist attempted to give her hope by singing, "This little light of mine, I'm gonna let it shine." Spontaneously, Giffords joined in, effortlessly repeating the word "light" over and over again in the song. These types of breakthroughs are common and show music's magical ability to survive brain damage and degeneration. When you can't speak, you can often still sing.

Music therapists use this fact to treat various conditions, from aphasia to Parkinson's disease. Music bypasses our central executive, who can sometimes get stuck in a rut. In Parkinson's disease, for example, patients have trouble initiating voluntary movements. One patient described it to me as a truly bizarre experience. When he wants to take a step, he tells his legs to do it, but now, half the time, they just ignore him. But when he goes to dance class or walks while listening to music, his legs just do their thing. His ineffective central executive gets bypassed by the power of music.

A similar thing happens with speech in people who, like Giffords, have trouble talking after traumatic brain injuries or strokes (this condition is called Broca's aphasia). Music therapists use a technique called Melodic Intonation Therapy, where they intone words and have patients repeat them while beating out a rhythm with their left hand.

The rhythm and melody help patients produce the sounds that eluded them. Therapists start with particularly useful phrases like "My name is Harry" or "Where is the bathroom?" They sing these phrases in short melodies which the patients memorize. Then, in social situations, patients can draw on these melodies to speak the phrases. Melodic Intonation Therapy makes a patient's speech more intelligible and natural, even when she isn't singing.

How does it work? It seems to tap into the brain's superpower: neuroplasticity. We used to think that once you reached adulthood, physical changes in the brain were limited. But a growing body of evidence shows that the brain does change later in life. Pretty dramatically, too, with time and experience. Musical training is a poster child of neuroplasticity because it's so effective at causing measurable changes in the anatomy of the brain.

For most people, most aspects of language are localized in the left hemisphere, with the exception of musical components, such as prosody, which are more commonly in the right hemisphere. When a stroke or a traumatic brain injury damages left frontal lobes, Melodic Intonation Therapy helps create a new pathway for language in the analogous regions of the right hemisphere.

Specifically, a white matter tract called the arcuate fasciculus (say that five times quickly) joins the part of the left temporal lobe where speech comprehension is localized (Wernicke's area) with the part of the left frontal lobe that's critical for speech production (Broca's area). There's an equivalent tract in the right hemisphere, but in most people, it's much smaller.

In patients who have undergone Melodic Intonation Therapy, however, the arcuate fasciculus in the *right* hemisphere grows, which might be how the therapeutic technique paves a new route for language production.

Not all patients benefit from therapy. It seems to depend largely on exactly which regions are damaged and which spared. But there is a growing list of promising music therapy treatments for different types of patients. And there's been a surge of interest in bringing music into health care, so I only expect these treatments to grow in number and efficacy.

It's not just brain-damaged patients who can benefit from music. Listening to music reduces anxiety in coronary heart disease patients. It reduces the length of colonoscopies, which is good for everyone involved. Singing might even cause measurable boosts in immune system function in cancer patients, helping them fight off the disease. And the majority of operating room staff in one study agreed that music in the operating theater helps them relax, which has to be a good thing, right?

One of the most-studied uses of music in health care has been to reduce pain and anxiety before and after invasive medical procedures. In about half of the studies, the effects of music are significantly better than a control condition, even than a dose of a benzodiazepine, a commonly used sedative. In some studies, doctors used smaller dosages of analgesics and sedatives when music was available to patients. Levels of the stress hormone cortisol have also been found to be lower in patients with a music intervention.

Why don't all the studies show music's effectiveness? One reason brings us right back to the beginning: Music is subjective. When a patient chooses her playlist, outcomes improve. When music is chosen for her, the data are mixed.

So how, exactly, does music ease pain and reduce anxiety? It comes down to three things: distraction, feeling good, and lowering stress.

When you're facing an unpleasant medical procedure, you're usually also subjected to unpleasant sounds— beeping machines, difficult conversations, other patients' distressed cries. Music provides an alternative sound-scape. You might also be ruminating on what's about to happen. Music can take your mind off the procedure.

Music also taps into your homemade pain-relief tools, increasing the levels of endogenous opioids in your brain. And it can make you smile. Together, these effects lead to good feelings.

Finally, music decreases levels of the stress hormone cortisol and lowers the activity of the amygdala, which is involved in anxiety.

Apparently it's not just humans who benefit. In a 2012 study, classical music helped kenneled dogs relax, too. Dogs exposed to it slept longer and vocalized less than dogs that weren't played music.

But all these effects are largely dependent on the type of music you're listening to and your musical preferences. Even dogs have tastes. Those exposed to heavy metal music weren't so relaxed, showing shaking behavior (a sign of nervousness) more often than dogs left in silence. But for monkeys, a piece by Metallica was calming, while Barber's *Adagio for Strings*, our human chill-inducing music, had no effect. So bring your own favorite playlist if you need to chill before a procedure.

Music can be a life preserver in the tumultuous sea of Alzheimer's disease, but once again, the best results occur when the music is curated for a particular patient.

The later stages of the disease often rob patients of the ability to communicate. They spend hours staring blankly, giving the impression that their minds are totally lost. But expose them to the music of their teenage years and they suddenly come alive: They sway to the music, sometimes singing along. Their faces are suddenly full of emotional expressions, and we once again glimpse the fullness of the person they once were. It's as though their conscious self has returned from some faraway place.

They also show measurable improvements on tests of cognitive function, like remembering details from their past, paying attention, and naming as many items as possible from a specific category, like animals or fruits. And just thirty minutes a day of listening to music that they love reduces their anxiety.

But perhaps most compelling is that music interventions help people with dementia regain a sense of community and make their lives feel meaningful again. Their self-esteem improves; they feel more competent and less alone. Which is not surprising if music gives them access to their conscious selves once again, enabling them to connect with others. And these benefits are not limited to patients with dementia, but can be seen in elderly people in general.

Singing, moving, connecting. Music gives us one more chance to be ourselves, to share emotional experiences with caretakers and loved ones, to bring our minds back so the living soul glimmers in our eyes.

Why does music persist when much of the mind is lost? The answer remains a great mystery of neuroscience, but the fact that music is redundantly represented in multiple circuits, that it's intricately linked to memory, and that we feel connected to each other through music more directly than through speech are all clues. There's also some evidence that Alzheimer's spares the parts of the brain that activate when patients listen to familiar music, compared with unknown music.

We also see increased oxytocin in the brain when patients listen to music. Oxytocin is a neuropeptide sometimes called the "love hormone" because of its role in social attachment. It's more complicated than just love, as we'll explore later, but it might be how music helps patients and elderly people connect socially, and can do the same for the rest of us. For me, one of the greatest joys of singing is the connection with an audience. We enter the theater with a variety of opinions, beliefs, joys, and sorrows. But for a few minutes, when I feel the energy of the audience from the stage, I feel that there is much more that brings us together than separates us.

Soothing a baby to sleep with song is a universal use of music across cultures. But why does it work so well?

Singing to premature babies helps them leave the hospital sooner by improving their sleep and feeding quality, and even measurably reducing their heart rate and helping them breathe more deeply. And when caregivers sing lullabies to full-term babies, they cry less and show fewer symptoms of colic in the first three months after birth. No wonder lullabies are popular.

But babies aren't the only ones who benefit. The caregivers report feeling less stress when they sing to their charges. And pregnant women who are having trouble sleeping themselves experience improved sleep quality and less anxiety when they listen to lullabies for just two weeks.

This soporific feature of music extends to others who suffer from insomnia. A recent meta-analysis of twenty trials found that patients rank music as the most effective nonmedicinal intervention for falling asleep faster, and that music-assisted relaxation improved overall sleep quality.

If you're trying, and failing repeatedly, to fall asleep, it can be very frustrating. It's no surprise that the pleasure of listening to music, combined with overt relaxation suggestions, can send you off to a deeper sleep sooner. And falling asleep without medications gets you better quality zzz's.

What makes a lullaby such a powerful soother? Many of the thousands of different tunes used across the world share some common features. They often have a hypnotic quality, with lots of repetition and a simple melody. They frequently use a triple meter or 6/8 time signature, which evokes rocking or swinging, thought to mimic what it's like in the womb.

But another shared characteristic is a bit more surprising: The lyrics are often dark. Cradles falling from trees (English), demons woken up by crying (ancient Babylonian), babies soon to be eaten by hyenas (Kenyan), a wolf devouring a lamb (Italian), a baby torn into pieces by an eagle to punish its father for failing to sacrifice three camels (Turkish). Are these lyrics designed to teach babies the ways of the world? Or do they fit the moods of mothers suffering from the baby blues? Maybe lullabies are as much for the caregivers as for the babies.

Of course, music can also give you energy rather than soothing you to sleep. It's hard to find a gym that doesn't pipe energetic music through its speakers. And if you're used to running to a playlist, running in silence makes your legs ten times heavier. But does music improve your athletic performance, or is it simply a distraction from a difficult task?

Scientific data are equivocal. Some studies show that people are more motivated when listening to music, and they certainly rate the workout as more enjoyable and less effortful. Music can make your energy consumption more efficient and your time trials faster. If you ride or run to the music, you use less oxygen. And if you're pumping iron, listening to music you've picked out yourself can increase muscle power. High-intensity interval training seems to benefit significantly, in both enjoyment and peak power.

Boosting your playlist's tempo can make you pedal or run faster and work harder—you still feel the exertion, but don't mind it as much. Music can increase your self-esteem, keeping you aroused and interested, and distracting you from counting the minutes.

It might also assuage performance anxiety. In one study, a group of free-throw basketball shooters who were prone to choking under pressure performed better and were less self-aware after listening to the Monty Python song "Always Look on the Bright Side of Life." It's hard to take yourself too seriously when primed by the silliness of the surreal comedy troupe.

But when you're already at your limit, it seems music has little or no effect. Runners at 90 percent of their max don't do any better with music. And sprinters don't benefit from music as much as long-distance runners do.

But music still makes the workout more enjoyable, which makes you more likely to do it again. For my own workouts, I fully appreciate the distraction effect. But I also use exercise as a lab for discovering music, often taking classes with a playlist that is new to me.

We tend to think that music always improves our mood. But the relationship between music and mood isn't so straightforward—as Barber's *Adagio for Strings*, the "saddest music ever written" but also the music most likely to give us the pleasurable chills, demonstrates. Even when music induces negative emotions, paradoxically, we feel better. Is the sadness music brings really the same as the emotion induced by losing a loved one, failing at your job, or feeling depressed?

"Sad but true" is a more profound statement than it first appears: When we're sad, we tend to see life more clearly. This phenomenon is called *depressive realism*. Sadness makes us more detail oriented and less biased, and even helps us remember details better. And one study found that when we listen to sad music, we evaluate ourselves and the world more accurately.

But that's not the only reason we enjoy sad music. It's also neurochemical. The hormone prolactin is released specifically when we listen to sad music. Prolactin is associated with milk production in breastfeed-ing mothers; in people of all genders, it's released when we cry. It's also correlated with feelings of tranquility and well-being, which is perhaps why a good cry can be comforting.

What if you could have that comforting effect without the discomfort of whatever made you cry? Listening to Adele work through her breakup pain can induce empathy and a release of prolactin. But then we remember we're not the ones suffering, and we find the comfort a net positive gain in our mood—and that feels good.

It's no secret that turning a list of facts into a song makes them easier to memorize. Who among us didn't learn the alphabet that way? It's effective because it gives you more cues with which to retrieve the material. It also provides a sequence for remembering—one thing leads to the next. And music is represented in multiple pathways in the brain, so if you lose access to one, there are other routes to the information.

Music therapists and educators have also effectively used music to help kids with special needs. Music therapy has helped children on the autism spectrum communicate and learn. And kids with dyslexia can improve their language skills more quickly with musical interventions.

Listening to and making music teaches children how to extract meaning from sound. Improvisational music making also teaches them turn taking, eye contact, listening, and response—key social skills that often challenge children on the autism spectrum. And music helps students connect with their teachers and caregivers, infusing joy into lessons.

That's why teachers find that setting core curriculum items to music is almost sure to boost test scores. Students are more engaged during lessons, encode information more elaborately, and have more routes to retrieval when faced with an exam.

But can music make kids generally smarter? You might have heard that listening to Mozart is good for kids' and even babies' intelligence. Is that true?

The idea underlying the Mozart effect came from a study at the University of California, Irvine, published in 1993. While most current applications involve infants and toddlers, the study wasn't conducted on children at all. Instead, university undergraduate students were asked to complete tests of cognitive abilities, like rotating shapes in their mind's eye. Just before the tests, they did one of three things for ten minutes: sat in silence, listened to relaxation instructions, or listened to Mozart's Sonata for Two Pianos in D Major.

The students who listened to Mozart scored higher on tests of spatial cognition. But this enhancement lasted only a few minutes.

Then along came evidence of the Mozart effect in animals. In one study, rats were exposed to either Mozart's piano sonata, minimalist music by Philip Glass, white noise, or silence in utero and then postpartum for about sixty days. After the intervention, the Mozart group completed a maze test significantly more quickly and with fewer errors than the other three groups. It seems that Mozart works for rats too!

But later, scientists found that pop songs worked just as well, in undergraduates anyway. Even reading a Stephen King story worked. So the effect wasn't specific to Mozart—it was a general increase in arousal. Listening to music was more stimulating than sitting in silence or relaxing.

The rat finding is harder to interpret, as scientists don't think rodents find Mozart's music emotionally arousing. It might have to do with overlapping brain regions. Whether you're a rat or a human, brain regions involved in spatial reasoning (such as navigating a maze) overlap with those activated by music with specific patterns (like Mozart's). Maybe Mozartian music primes those regions in rats, so that when it's time to solve a puzzle, they're ready.

While listening to Mozart might not make you measurably smarter than reading a great novel would, long-term musical training—active participation rather than passive listening—*can* show many benefits beyond arousal. Infants as young as six months show accelerated social skill development with participatory music lessons, while prolonged individual lessons can leave measurable marks on the brain. Music can help battered women learn a second language in a foreign country. It can repair language deficits in children. And it can boost IQ—but only if you stick to it for at least eighteen months of individual lessons.

As we already learned, musical training is a canonical example of neuroplasticity in action. What exactly is neuroplasticity, and why is it so great?

For decades after the first pieces of evidence appeared, many neuroscientists refused to accept the idea that the adult brain can physically change in dramatic ways and even possibly grow new cells.

It takes decades to develop the adult brain because it is shaped by experience. So if you were to turn over your brain cells like you do your outer skin cells, essentially growing a new epidermis every forty-eight days, you'd never learn to speak, let alone read Tolstoy or play the cello. Since our cumulated knowledge is painstakingly wired into the brain over years and years, you can't just replace cells without dire consequences.

It doesn't make sense for the brain to be infinitely plastic, and scores of patients with brain damage who never recover certain functions seem to prove the point.

Then there's my godmother, Rita, who can recite hundreds of Lithuanian songs she learned as a child. Now I know she doesn't practice them every day, and decades can go by without her giving one a second thought, only to sing it without missing a beat at a gathering of old friends. How is that possible if the brain's cells are as malleable as Play-Doh?

Yet as few as fifteen months of weekly individual music lessons measurably changed the neuroanatomy of the sixth-graders who participated in a study, compared with their friends (matched for socioeconomic status) who just got one group lesson a week.

Not only does the brain's wiring change with experience even in adulthood, but it might even be possible to turn on new cell growth in two regions of the adult human brain. Whether we actually grow new neurons in adulthood remains hotly debated. But if it happens, the two regions showing neurogenesis are both involved in learning. One is in the hippocampus, which turns conscious short-term memories for facts and events into long-lasting ones. The other is the basal ganglia, which supports our habit and skill learning. We use these new cells to lay down new memories, but their wiring is local, so the changes don't disturb existing memories.

But neurogenesis isn't automatic in an adult brain the way it is in an infant brain—you need to turn it on. And while we're still figuring out how that works in humans (and, frankly, whether it works at all), we've found that in rodents, aerobic exercise followed by learning a difficult new skill is the winning recipe. And we see higher levels of brain-derived neurotrophic factor (a protein involved in neurogenesis) in adults who exercise more, so this might also apply to us. The catch is that you can boost the growth of those cells, but unless you struggle and successfully learn something new, the cells don't integrate into the brain. At least not if you're a rodent.

So what's a good thing to learn? Whatever you do to integrate useful new neurons has to be hard. And anyone who has picked up a new musical instrument late in life knows how hard it is.

We know that musical training changes brains. Musicians' brains show differences compared with nonmusicians' brains, and by mapping these differences, and demonstrating that more training yields bigger changes, we can see how music shapes the brain.

When we map musicians' brains, we see what we would expect, and some surprises. As expected, parts of the brain involved in processing sound and connecting auditory regions to motor regions are more developed. And the sensorimotor cortex, which enables us to feel and move our bodies a certain way, shows changes specific to an instrument and its corresponding body part—pianists' fingers or singers' throat muscles.

More surprising is that the corpus callosum (the fiber tract that connects the two hemispheres) is also larger in musicians. And long-term musical training also allows musicians to pronounce foreign languages more accurately and have better spatial-tactile acuity, like the kind necessary to read Braille.

The scope of these differences is one reason it's harder to master an instrument later in life—such changes don't happen as quickly as they do when you're young. But that's precisely why it might be *more* beneficial. Synaptogenesis, the growth of new connections between cells, is even more important as you age and are losing precious cells than when you're a child and they're sprouting up like weeds. Even healthy aging brings brain tissue loss, but adding connections between cells or even entirely new cells can stave off decline.

And it's not true that kids learn everything faster than adults. One study pitted kids aged six to ten against college-age adults on a button-pressing task—akin to playing the piano or a video game. To the surprise of the experimenters, the adults consistently learned new sequences with fewer tries than the kids. What makes kids better learners might not be their plastic brains but their persistence, and different strategies, which any motivated adult can match.

Not all plasticity is desirable, however. Some musicians develop a condition called focal dystonia, or musician's cramp. One of my students is an excellent clarinettist, and her dystonia made it hard for her to move her pinkie and ring fingers independently, because they so often move in sync when she plays. This type of "injury" is common, even among some of the greatest musicians, like country blues musician Charlie Parr, pianist Leon Fleisher, oboist Alex Klein, and Stuart Cassells of the Red Hot Chili Peppers.

The cramping and movements suggest the problem is in the affected area. But it's a plasticity problem in the brain. When two previously separate body parts like the ring finger and the pinkie are repetitively used together, the brain begins to represent them as one thing rather than two. The musician must then begin the painstaking and often emotional process of unlearning and relearning a skill that they have poured heart and soul into developing. So have they practiced a bit too much? 10,001 hours instead of the required 10,000? And are all those hours created equal? Let's turn to that question next.

When you watch a skilled musician play, it's easy to think some people are just born talented. Some musicians play their instruments so precisely and gracefully that our listening brains can barely keep up.

And if you've suffered through years of piano lessons and still can't play that one piece that you've always wanted to, then you're even more sure that musical genius is bestowed, not earned. Maybe you know someone who improved much faster than you did. Or who could pick up any instrument and play it reasonably well without any lessons.

I certainly believed in talent as I watched some singers seemingly effortlessly master a difficult aria that I'd been working on for months.

But it's next to impossible to compare one person's potential with another's. Brains are shaped by all kinds of experiences, even as early as in the womb. And all these factors make it difficult to study talent and effort scientifically. I like to say that talent is just the part of what separates individual performers that we don't understand yet.

Certainly some physical traits give musicians an edge: better hearing, better dexterity, larger hands for pianists, bigger heads for opera singers. Some of these traits are largely determined by genes. And even psychological traits like determination, grit, and motivation seem to run in families.

But we often underestimate how much our experiences can shape cognitive and even physical traits. For most kids, adding fish oil supplements to their diets doesn't measurably impact reading or other skills. But for kids who are malnourished and from low-income backgrounds, one little pill a day can make a big difference in their cognitive development. Genes don't act in a vacuum.

A child's ability to find meaning in sound is shaped not just by genes but also by the early environment. If you grew up in a city, where you had to tune out car horns and garbage trucks, you trained your brain to ignore certain sounds. If you were raised in a quiet house, brought to life on Sunday afternoons when the family gathered around the record player, you likely learned to listen greedily and thoughtfully to music.

Musicians train to extract meaning from a complex soundscape. This training changes how they hear not just music, but other sounds as well. They are better at picking out speech in noisy environments, for example, and this ability continues to improve with more musical practice.

So a kid with early exposure to music will hear better than a child without such experience. That difference can give one child an edge, before she takes a single music lesson.

By the same token, not every practice hour is created equal. You can sit with a violin for hours, trying very hard to make it sound good, but without the knowledgeable instruction of a great teacher, you won't get very far.

Anders Ericsson, whose research helped coin the 10,000-hours rule, points out how important having a good teacher can be. To become a master in anything, you need to surpass most of your competition and ultimately even your teachers. In domains without a collective expertise—some obscure or new skill, such as piloting a drone or completing a Rubik's Cube blindfolded—you might not need anywhere close to 10,000 hours of practice to become a world champion. But as the skill catches on, the competition gets tougher, and good teachers emerge with more effective training techniques, the number of hours required to master it increases.

There's an often-told story about a violin concerto written by Pyotr Ilyich Tchaikovsky in 1878. Leopold Auer, the star violinist to whom the piece was dedicated, called it "unplayable." These days, most professional solo violinists keep the piece in their repertoire, and it's hard to build a successful solo career without tackling it. Scientists who study expertise point to this story to show how much violin training has advanced over the last 150 years.

But this story is not without a controversy. In a 1912 interview, Leopold Auer explained:

> It is incorrect to state that I had declared the concerto in its original form unplayable. What I did say was that some of the passages were not suited to the character of the instrument, and that, however perfectly rendered, they would not sound as well as the composer had imagined. From this purely aesthetic point of view only I found some of it impracticable, and for this reason I re-edited the solo part.

Sometimes musicians make choices for artistic rather than technical reasons. And how do we compare one talent with another if artistry is subjective?

When it comes to overcoming technical challenges, though, how a person practices can make the difference. Anyone who has developed a complex skill has likely come face-to-face with the power law of learning: Gains are rapid at first, but the better you get, the harder you have to work to get even better. Sometimes it feels like all the practice in the world won't get you over the hump.

There's some truth to that. In a 2014 study, scientists found that deliberate practice time only accounts for about 21 percent of the variability between musicians' skills. What about the other 79 percent? Is that where genes come in? Maybe in part. But there's another factor that I alluded to earlier: It's what happens during those hours of training that separates the masters from the dilettantes.

The authors of such studies rely largely on self-reported practice hours. But what a person does during an hour of practice varies widely. Ericsson, an expert on expertise, distinguishes purposeful from deliberate practice.

Purposeful practice is what most people engage in when they want to learn a new skill. They focus on what they want to improve, methodically work on exercises, and make great strides at first but eventually plateau. If they don't find a good teacher, they stop improving and often quit.

The right teacher helps you punch through a plateau by identifying your obstacles and telling you how to overcome them. This is the first step in making purposeful practice deliberate. Finding the right teacher might be far more important than the number of hours you spend in the practice room.

Ericsson has found that the best deliberate practice includes five features: (1) leaving your comfort zone and entering a place where mistakes are likely; (2) working toward specific, achievable goals; (3) maintaining intensive focus on the task; (4) getting high-quality feedback and opportunities to correct errors in the moment; and (5) developing a new mental model of the skill you're trying to master.

Even the most diligent of us will struggle to meet all five requirements in every practice hour. But integrating some of these features can make one person's hours much more effective than another's.

Another factor that makes a difference is our motivation, or how we approach practice. Carol Dweck and her colleagues have shown how beliefs about intelligence—specifically, whether it's learned or innate—can have far-reaching effects on motivation and other aspects of a child's life, including mitigating the effects of poverty on academic achievement. She calls these beliefs "mindsets."

Kids who are praised for achievement, who get straight A's, or who are considered musical prodigies often develop a belief that their intelligence or talent is fixed and innate. These kids avoid taking risks. They see effort as a sign of weakness. When criticized, they feel hurt and focus on their emotions rather than on the content of the criticism. We even see brain activation in emotional processing areas rather than memory-related ones.

But kids who are praised for their effort or who have worked hard to learn a new skill often develop a growth mindset—a belief that if they put the effort in, they can improve. They see effort as a path to mastery. They set learning rather than performance goals, like understanding a mathematical concept or playing a difficult piece, not acing a test or winning a competition. They take risks, show greater persistence, and even enjoy practicing or studying. When criticized, they are more likely to correct their mistakes in the future. They show more memory-related brain activation and get less emotionally distraught when faced with criticism.

Bringing a growth mindset into the practice room and leaving notions of fixed talent at the door might contribute to the remaining 79 percent of variability among individuals. If every wrong note makes you question your self-worth, practice is excruciating. But if you approach each hour as another step toward mastery, those 10,000 hours will be more effective, and they will fly by.

And one thing that I've learned both by studying and by teaching others is that practice, just like the skill you're working on, can always be improved. Bringing a variety of strategies into play makes the work much more enjoyable and even creative. Which, after all, is the whole point.

PART 3

HOW CAN MUSIC MAKE SOCIETY BETTER?

Music is almost always social—except on the rare occasions when the composer, performer, and intended listener are all the same person. And music can be powerful social glue, bringing people together in rituals, ceremonies, marches, protests, concerts, and more.

One way music binds people together is by harnessing empathy. When you listen to music that moves you, the activation in your brain mimics what is happening in the performers' brains. This mirroring underlies our ability to put ourselves in someone else's shoes—to empathize. And playing music with others makes kids more empathetic.

The overlap between the brains of listeners and performers isn't just in areas that process sound. We also see comparable activation in the anterior insula. This region is involved in understanding our feelings and thoughts and those of others. When you bring your awareness to your heartbeat, for example, or when you watch someone enduring pain and imagine what it would be like, the insular cortex is engaged.

Listening to emotional music and feeling empathy and compassion both involve the insula. But the more familiar you are with the music, and how it would feel were you the one playing it, the more similar your brain activation is to the performers'. Pianists listening to other pianists show not only auditory and higher cortical activation, but also activation in the motor cortex, as if they were playing the piano themselves. When choirs sing in sync, their breathing and heart rates entrain too. Synchrony isn't just in the sound waves; it's in brain waves too.

When we share a physical and emotional experience, we form social bonds and behave more compassionately. When people move in sync to music, they later report liking and trusting each other more. They also remember more about each other and are more likely to cooperate, compared with a control group of adults who move in the same way but not in sync. For example, when participants in an experiment played the drums along with the experimenter, they were more likely to help her pick up a bunch of pencils that she "accidentally" dropped at the end of the study.

Can sharing a musical experience tame even a toddler? Infants as young as fourteen months who were bounced by an adult in synchrony to music were more likely to help the adult pick up "accidentally" dropped objects than infants who were bounced out of sync. Interestingly, this effect extended to "friends" of the adult but not to neutral strangers. Just as music can bind us together, it can also separate us from other groups or tribes.

Oxytocin, the neuropeptide that, through music, can help anyone (especially the elderly and people with dementia) feel less isolated, is involved in building trust, cooperation, parenting, empathy, and other prosocial behaviors. And its levels increase in the brain during choral singing and other musical activities. What's more, if you give people a little boost of oxytocin, they are better at tapping in sync with each other. It gives them rhythm.

But it also might be the reason why music can be divisive. Oxytocin isn't just about love; it can also induce hate. Let's turn to that paradox next.

Music doesn't just affect individual brains—it can shape entire civilizations. From work songs sung by our Paleolithic ancestors to anthems that incite revolutions today, music can build or destroy communities. Even Charles Darwin recognized music's ability to shape humanity, as a precursor to language—arguably the one thing that separates us from all other animals.

> [It] appears probable that the progenitors of man, either the males or females or both sexes, before acquiring the power of expressing their mutual love in articulate language, endeavoured to charm each other with musical notes and rhythm. The impassioned orator, bard, or musician, when with his varied tones and cadences he excites the strongest emotions in his hearers, little suspects that he uses the same means by which his half-human ancestors long ago aroused each other's ardent passions, during their courtship and rivalry.

We have yet to discover a culture that does not or did not practice music. Caregivers all over the world sing to their infants, making music one of the first things a newborn hears. Anniversaries, religious ceremonies, political assemblies, parties, and other social gatherings almost always include music. People frequently rank music as one of the top things that bring them pleasure—above food, money, and visual art, according to one set of studies.

Music can mobilize people to support causes. Just look at the success of benefit concerts. When George Harrison joined forces with Ravi Shankar in 1971, their concert raised $250,000 for refugees from what was about to become Bangladesh. Once the live album and film were released, that amount jumped to about $12 million.

By adding music to a benefit, organizers tap into music's power to make us feel bonded, especially to celebrities we admire. If we donate to their cause, doesn't that make us feel that we're part of their tribe?

Music can also incite action by giving us an unforgettable slogan, embedded in the memory-enhancing power of rhythm, melody, and emotion. Bob Marley's "Get Up, Stand Up" makes even the most indolent couch potato want to move.

But does listening to inspirational music sometimes back-fire? Can we feel the emotional rush so strongly that we think we've done enough, without actually making the change the music calls for? Having sung the song for five years, Marley reportedly asked, "How long must I protest the same thing?" In the book *Bob Marley: In His Own Words*, he is quoted as saying, "I sing 'Get up, Stand Up' and up 'til now, people don't get up. So I must still sing. . . ."

The song remains an anthem for preserving human rights internationally; yet Haiti, which inspired it, remains one of the poorest countries in the world. Musicians will find it just as inspiring a place to write a protest song today as Marley did in the early 1970s.

Perhaps poverty and inequality are too big to fix with music. What about civil rights in America? Billie Holiday's rendition of "Strange Fruit" is still one of the most poignant protests of racism, detailing the barbaric practice of lynching. As a poem, the lyrics are moving; but it wasn't until she began singing the song that its full power was unleashed. For some scholars, it marks the beginning of the American civil rights movement, sixteen years before Rosa Parks refused to give up her seat.

John Lennon's "Imagine" depicts a world at peace, devoid of nationalist or religious conflicts. It's one of the most performed songs of the twentieth century. But the lyrics ask the listener to accept something unpalatable for many people: no possessions, no nationality, no religion. If the same words were spoken, would so many people love them? How does setting these controversial views to a lilting melody make us more likely to endorse them? Do they lose their subversive power? Are we lulled into agreeing with the singer because it sounds nice? Sometimes, enjoying a melody opens us up to an idea that's difficult to swallow. The empathy we feel for the musicians, based in part on how their performance taps into our brains, can blind us to the consequences of their message.

Perhaps music is more effective at inciting violence than creating world peace. A testament to music's power to mobilize fighters is Bono's insistence that "Sunday Bloody Sunday" is "not a rebel song." It depicts a horrific incident in Northern Ireland when British troops killed unarmed protesters and bystanders. Bono was so worried that the song would lead to more violence, despite the lyrics that explicitly call for peace, that he hesitated to perform in public what became one of his most popular pieces.

Is this fear justified? There is evidence that listening to violent songs primes us to interpret ambiguous words and word fragments aggressively (like filling in "h_t" with an "i" rather than an "a") and to have more aggressive feelings and thoughts. But do these effects translate into actions? Or do songs help us work through aggression? "Get Up, Stand Up" hasn't rid Haiti of poverty; does violent music really breed more violence?

One of the most beautiful stories of how music can be used to comfort rather than confront comes from one of the most atrocious times in human history: the Holocaust. Adults preceding their children to the gas chambers sang to comfort their little ones. But the Nazis also used music to torture and humiliate prisoners in concentration camps, and to motivate soldiers to carry out inhuman orders. Like any powerful tool in the wrong hands, music can be dangerous. And it can also bring meaning to our darkest moments.

Darwin thought music was a gift from natural selection, ensuring the propagation of musical genes. Linguist Steven Pinker disagrees in *How the Mind Works*: "I suspect music is auditory cheesecake, an exquisite confection crafted to tickle the sensitive spots of . . . our mental faculties."

Pinker argues that our language abilities were selected for, and music came along for the ride. So which came first, music or language? Are our brains predisposed to consume music or does music simply take advantage of a brain wired for language?

We may never answer that question definitively but, either way, music influences us profoundly. Whether it's releasing stress, improving mood, powering a workout, comforting through grief, dulling pain, cueing memory, or connecting us in an ever more isolationist society, music is great. Even when it's not "great."

Does music also make our genes more likely to survive and reproduce? Has it shaped our species through evolution? To have been selected for in our evolutionary history, music wouldn't have had to make us better predators or survivors. Like the peacock's tail, an adaptation doesn't have to directly influence our survival.

In Darwin's view, music in humans evolved in response to *sexual* selection—just as it did in songbirds.

Traits that proliferate through sexual selection don't enhance survival, but rather demonstrate fitness to potential mates. A peacock that drags around a glorious tail all day long must be pretty good at other things related to staying alive. Otherwise it wouldn't live very long. Likewise, a particularly creative songbird can afford to spend time crafting the perfect love song, since finding food and shelter and avoiding predators is a breeze. And female birds do prefer good crooners. Is this also why humans flock to sexy rock stars? Is music all about selecting a better mate?

Proponents of this hypothesis point to the apparent sexual attractiveness of rock stars like Jimi Hendrix (though not often female examples like Beyoncé or Madonna). If you're so rich that you can spend all your resources developing your talent, you must be well-endowed, genetically speaking.

Geoffrey Miller, at University College London, insists that the "principal biological function of music, then, is sexual courtship." But perhaps this hypothesis is too steeped in a patriarchal view of our evolutionary origins. Reducing all music to seduction misses out on all the other ways it can affect us. Maybe this view reflects the culture of the scientists, rather than that of our ancestors.

Still, the sexual selection argument is supported by music's importance in social bonds. This brings us back to the neuropeptide oxytocin, whose levels increase in our brains when we're affected by music. A lesser-known fact about oxytocin is that its effects are selective: It can lubricate social bonds between tribespeople, but it can also make us more aggressive toward our perceived enemies. John Lennon would not approve. In the musical *West Side Story*, the white Jets get all riled up and ready to fight the Puerto Rican Sharks when they sing their "Jet Song," which not only solidifies their bonds but also builds aggression toward the rival gang.

Outside of fiction, music is often used to taunt rival gangs, as the famous battles between East and West Coast hip-hop artists demonstrate.

But to understand how music evolved, we have to look at the conditions that our ancestors faced during the Stone Age. The oldest instruments we've found are around 40,000 years old, and singing and other ways of making music with our bodies almost certainly originated earlier. Maybe musical prowess was selected for when we needed to coordinate our actions in a work setting, for example. If I need to move a big rock (it was, after all, the Stone Age), I might gesture to a buddy and say something like "1, 2, 3, go!" And rhythm is born. Singing while working is common in many cultures—from fieldwork songs to sea shanties.

Or maybe music wasn't selected for by evolution at all. Maybe it emerged as a technological innovation like fire, as Ani Patel suggests. Fire enabled us to cook and therefore spend less time searching for and digesting food. That left more time for contemplating our place in the universe, so that we began to understand the laws of physics, among other things. Gorillas have smaller brains even though their bodies are bigger, largely because they subsist on a raw food diet and simply can't get enough nutrition to fuel a larger brain.

A later innovation, reading and writing, gave us other cognitive abilities and helped us share information, enabling major leaps in civilization. But music comes before the ability to read—both developmentally and evolutionarily. Maybe its cognitive benefits in children are no accident. Maybe they are the reason it has become such a universal feature of humanity. Maybe music played, and continues to play, a key role in the development of our complex minds. This idea brings us back to the Mozart effect and music's effects on intelligence and social abilities.

Given these benefits, I think it's particularly sad that our society is shifting away from a model in which everyone performs music and toward a model in which a few people make music and the rest of us consume it. As David Byrne laments in *How Music Works*, the recording industry has largely replaced instruments in the home with sound systems. The amateur musician, who used to roam the plains in the millions, is becoming endangered.

My own genre, opera, is a case in point. In Italy, even in the smallest towns, opera used to be for the masses. Any random young person could sing a famous aria or two. And that's just what many of those pieces were written for—especially in the nineteenth century. Operas were full of great tunes designed to help people pass the time.

But now, most people wouldn't dream of trying to learn an aria without the watchful eye of a teacher. Sure, singing opera well enough to enthrall discerning audiences requires years of practice. But the joy of singing timeless melodies is available to everyone. We've just been conditioned to expect perfection. When you've grown up listening only to Luciano Pavarotti, it's no surprise that you wouldn't dare crack open "Nessun Dorma." But if most of your nights out ended with friends belting it out after a few pints, mangled words, cracked high notes, and all, it wouldn't seem so out of reach.

Why should we bring back the amateur, if we have access to greats like Pavarotti, Nina Simone, and Louis Armstrong on our smartphones? Being an amateur can be very liberating. And one of music's great powers is the release of tension. We can all benefit from performing music. It has redemptive power, as the popularity of shows like *The Voice* and *America's Got Talent* demonstrate. The story of the Welsh coal miner who can sing opera or the mousy girl from Brixton whose first album went platinum give us hope that our own beautiful souls will someday escape the mundane trap of our lives. And we can't take advantage of all the ways that music shapes our brains if we restrict ourselves to listening. It's playing music, not simply listening, that unlocks our potential for widespread neuroplasticity.

Music is
and always should be
for everyone.
It can make us all better.

Altenmüller, E. (2010). Focal dystonia in musicians: Phenome-
nology, pathophysiology, triggering factors, and treatment.
Medical Problems of Performing Artists, 25(1), 3–9.

Anderson, C. A., N. L. Carnagey, and J. Eubanks (2003).
Exposure to violent media: The effects of songs with
violent lyrics on aggressive thoughts and feelings. *Journal of
Personality and Social Psychology, 84*(5), 960.

Ashley, R. (2002). Do[n't] change a hair for me: The art of jazz
rubato. *Music Perception: An Interdisciplinary Journal, 19*(3),
311–332.

Babiloni, C., P. Buffo, F. Vecchio, N. Marzano, C. Del Percio,
D. Spada, . . . and D. Perani (2012). Brains "in concert":
Frontal oscillatory alpha rhythms and empathy in profes-
sional musicians. *Neuroimage, 60*(1), 105–116.

Baker, F., and E. A. Roth (2004). Neuroplasticity and functional
recovery: Training models and compensatory strategies
in music therapy. *Nordic Journal of Music Therapy, 13*(1),
20–32.

Barnason, S., L. Zimmerman, and J. Nieveen (1995). The
effects of music interventions on anxiety in the patient after
coronary artery bypass grafting. *Heart & Lung: The Journal
of Acute and Critical Care, 24*(2), 124–132.

Barrett, K. C., R. Ashley, D. L. Strait, and N. Kraus (2013).
Art and science: how musical training shapes the brain.
Frontiers in Psychology, 4, 713.

Beaman, C. P., and T. I. Williams (2010). Earworms (stuck song syndrome): Towards a natural history of intrusive thoughts. *British Journal of Psychology, 101*(4), 637–653.

Bechtold, M. L., S. R. Puli, M. O. Othman, C. R. Bartalos, J. B. Marshall, and P. K. Roy (2009). Effect of music on patients undergoing colonoscopy: a meta-analysis of randomized controlled trials. *Digestive Diseases and Sciences, 54*(1), 19–24.

Berlyne, D. E. (1971). *Aesthetics and Psychobiology.* New York: Appleton-Century-Crofts.

Biagini, M. S., L. E. Brown, J. W. Coburn, D. A. Judelson, T. A. Statler, M. Bottaro, . . . and N. A. Longo (2012). Effects of self-selected music on strength, explosiveness, and mood. *The Journal of Strength & Conditioning Research, 26*(7), 1934–1938.

Biederman, I., and E. A. Vessel (2006). Perceptual pleasure and the brain: A novel theory explains why the brain craves information and seeks it through the senses. *American Scientist, 94*(3), 247–253.

Blood, A. J., and R. J. Zatorre (2001). Intensely pleasurable responses to music correlate with activity in brain regions implicated in reward and emotion. *Proceedings of the National Academy of Sciences, 98*(20), 11818–11823.

Brown, J. D., and T. A. Mankowski (1993). Self-esteem, mood, and self-evaluation: Changes in mood and the way you see you. *Journal of Personality and Social Psychology, 64*(3), 421.

Brown, S., and J. Jordania (2013). Universals in the world's musics. *Psychology of Music,* 41: 229–248.

Byrne, D. (2012). *How Music Works.* San Francisco: McSweeney's.

Cepeda, M. S., D. B. Carr, J. Lau, and H. Alvarez (2006). Music for pain relief. *Cochrane Database Syst Rev, 2*(2).

Chanda, M. L., and D. J. Levitin (2013). The neurochemistry of music. *Trends in Cognitive Sciences, 17*(4), 179–193.

Cirelli, L. K., S. J. Wan, and L. J. Trainor (2014). Fourteen-month-old infants use interpersonal synchrony as a cue to direct helpfulness. *Philosophical Transactions of the Royal Society B: Biological Sciences, 369*(1658), 20130400.

Claro, S., D. Paunesku, and C. S. Dweck (2016). Growth mindset tempers the effects of poverty on academic achievement. *Proceedings of the National Academy of Sciences, 113*(31), 8664–8668.

Clements-Cortès, A. (2012). Neurologic music therapy: Music to influence and potentially change the brain. *Canadian Music Educator, 54*(1), 37–39.

Cochrane, T. (2010). A simulation theory of musical expressivity. *Australasian Journal of Philosophy, 88*(2), 191–207.

Cooke, M., W. Moyle, D. Shum, S. Harrison, and J. Murfield (2010). A randomized controlled trial exploring the effect of music on quality of life and depression in older people with dementia. *Journal of Health Psychology, 15*(5), 765–776.

Cross, H. A., C. G. Halcomb, and W. W. Matter (1967). Imprinting or exposure learning in rats given early auditory stimulation. *Psychonomic Science, 7*(7), 233–234.

Cross, I., and I. Morley (2009). The evolution of music: Theories, definitions and the nature of the evidence. In *Communicative Musicality: Exploring the Basis of Human Companionship*, edited by S. Malloch and C. Trevathen. Oxford: University Press, 61–81.

Dansby, A. (2002). Country scribe Harlan Howard dies. *Rolling Stone*. Retrieved from https://www.rollingstone.com/music/news/country-scribe-harlan-howard-dies-20020305.

Darwin, C. (1871). *The Descent of Man and Selection in Relation to Sex* (Vol. 1). London: Murray, 367.

De Dreu, C. K., S. Shalvi, L. L. Greer, G. A. Van Kleef, and M. J. Handgraaf (2012). Oxytocin motivates non-cooperation in intergroup conflict to protect vulnerable in-group members. *PLoS ONE, 7*(11), e46751.

De Dreu, M. J., A. S. D. Van Der Wilk, E. Poppe, G. Kwakkel, and E. E. van Wegen (2012). Rehabilitation, exercise therapy and music in patients with Parkinson's disease: A meta-analysis of the effects of music-based movement therapy on walking ability, balance and quality of life. *Parkinsonism & Related Disorders, 18*, S114–S119.

Deutsch, D., T. Henthorn, and R. Lapidis (2011). Illusory transformation from speech to song. *Journal of the Acoustical Society of America, 129*, 2245–2252.

Du, Y., N. C. Valentini, M. J. Kim, J. Whitall, and J. E. Clark (2017). Children and adults both learn motor sequences quickly, but do so differently. *Frontiers in Psychology, 8*, 158.

Dubé, L., and J. Le Bel (2003). The content and structure of laypeople's concept of pleasure. *Cognition & Emotion, 17*(2), 263–295.

Dweck, C. S. (2006). *Mindset: The New Psychology of Success*. New York: Random House.

Ericsson, K. A. (2006). The influence of experience and deliberate practice on the development of superior expert performance. *The Cambridge Handbook of Expertise and Expert Performance, 38*, 685–705.

Ericsson, K. A., R. T. Krampe, and C. Tesch-Römer (1993). The role of deliberate practice in the acquisition of expert performance. *Psychological Review, 100*(3), 363.

Ericsson, K. A., and R. Pool (2016). *Peak: Secrets from the New Science of Expertise.* Boston: Houghton Mifflin Harcourt.

Fancourt, D., A. Williamon, L. A. Carvalho, A. Steptoe, R. Dow, and I. Lewis (2016). Singing modulates mood, stress, cortisol, cytokine and neuropeptide activity in cancer patients and carers. *Ecancermedicalscience, 10*, 631.

Feng, F., Y. Zhang, J. Hou, J. Cai, Q. Jiang, X. Li, . . . and B. A. Li (2018). Can music improve sleep quality in adults with primary insomnia? A systematic review and network meta-analysis. *International Journal of Nursing Studies, 77*, 189–196.

Foerde, K., J. E. Steinglass, D. Shohamy, and B. T. Walsh (2015). Neural mechanisms supporting maladaptive food choices in anorexia nervosa. *Nature Neuroscience, 18*(11), 1571.

Gebauer, L., M. L. Kringelbach, and P. Vuust (2012). Ever-changing cycles of musical pleasure: The role of dopamine and anticipation. *Psychomusicology: Music, Mind and Brain, 22*(2), 152–167.

Gerry, D., A. Unrau, and L. J. Trainor (2012). Active music classes in infancy enhance musical, communicative and social development. *Developmental Science, 15*(3), 398–407.

Grahn, J. A., and M. Brett (2007). Rhythm and beat perception in motor areas of the brain. *Journal of Cognitive Neuroscience, 19*(5), 893–906.

Grahn, J. A., and J. B. Rowe (2009). Feeling the beat: Premotor and striatal interactions in musicians and nonmusicians during beat perception. *Journal of Neuroscience, 29*(23), 7540–7548.

Greenberg, R. On the *Cadence*: Season 1, Episode 5: Why Do We Like the Music That We Like? Air Date: April 13, 2017. http://theensembleproject.com/cadence/

Hambrick, D. Z., and E. M. Tucker-Drob (2015). The genetics of music accomplishment: Evidence for gene–environment correlation and interaction. *Psychonomic Bulletin & Review, 22*(1), 112–120.

Hove, M. J., and J. L. Risen (2009). It's all in the timing: Interpersonal synchrony increases affiliation. *Social Cognition, 27*(6), 949–960.

Huron, D. (2001). Is music an evolutionary adaptation? *Biological Foundations of Music,* 930: 43–61.

Huron, D. (2006). *Sweet anticipation: Music and the psychology of expectation.* Cambridge: MIT Press.

Huron, D. (2011). Why is sad music pleasurable? A possible role for prolactin. *Musicae Scientiae, 15*(2), 146–158.

Hyde, K. L., J. Lerch, A. Norton, M. Forgeard, E. Winner, A. C. Evans, and G. Schlaug (2009). The effects of musical training on structural brain development. *Annals of the New York Academy of Sciences, 1169*(1), 182–186.

Jacobsen, J. H., J. Stelzer, T. H. Fritz, G. Chételat, R. La Joie, and R. Turner (2015). Why musical memory can be preserved in advanced Alzheimer's disease. *Brain, 138*(8), 2438–2450.

Jarvis, E. D. (2007). Neural systems for vocal learning in birds and humans: A synopsis. *Journal of Ornithology, 148*(1), 35–44.

Jarvis, E. D., O. Güntürkün, L. Bruce, A. Csillag, H. Karten, W. Kuenzel, . . . and G. Striedter (2005). Avian brains and a new understanding of vertebrate brain evolution. *Nature Reviews Neuroscience, 6*(2), 151.

Karageorghis, C. I., and D. L. Priest (2012). Music in the exercise domain: A review and synthesis (Part II). *International Review of Sport and Exercise Psychology, 5*(1), 67–84.

Koelsch, S. (2014). Brain correlates of music-evoked emotions. *Nature Reviews Neuroscience, 15*(3), 170.

Koelsch, S., T. Fritz, D. Y. von Cramon, K. Müller, and A. D. Friederici (2006). Investigating emotion with music: An fMRI study. *Human Brain Mapping, 27*(3), 239–250.

Kogan, L. R., R. Schoenfeld-Tacher, and A. A. Simon (2012). Behavioral effects of auditory stimulation on kenneled dogs. *Journal of Veterinary Behavior: Clinical Applications and Research, 7*(5), 268–275.

Koger, S. M., K. Chapin, and M. Brotons (1999). Is music therapy an effective intervention for dementia? A meta-analytic review of literature. *Journal of Music Therapy, 36*(1), 2–15.

Kraus, N., and K. Banai (2007). Auditory-processing malleability: Focus on language and music. *Current Directions in Psychological Science, 16*(2), 105–110.

Kraus, N., and B. Chandrasekaran (2010). Music training for the development of auditory skills. *Nature Reviews Neuroscience, 11*(8), 599.

Leavitt, J. D., and N. J. Christenfeld (2011). Story spoilers don't spoil stories. *Psychological Science, 22*(9), 1152–1154.

Liikkanen, L. A. (2012). Musical activities predispose to involuntary musical imagery. *Psychology of Music, 40*(2), 236–256.

Loewy, J., K. Stewart, A. M. Dassler, A. Telsey, and P. Homel (2013). The effects of music therapy on vital signs, feeding, and sleep in premature infants. *Pediatrics, 131*(5), 902–918.

Macnamara, B. N., D. Z. Hambrick, and F. L. Oswald (2014). Deliberate practice and performance in music, games, sports, education, and professions: A meta-analysis. *Psychological Science, 25*(8), 1608–1618.

Margolick, D. (2013). *Strange Fruit: Billie Holiday, Café Society and an Early Cry for Civil Rights.* Edinburgh: Canongate Books.

Margulis, E. H. (2014). *On Repeat: How Music Plays the Mind.* Oxford: Oxford University Press.

Marley, B., and I. McCann (1993). *Bob Marley: In His Own Words.* London: Omnibus Press.

Mehr, S. A., M. Singh, H. York, L. Glowacki, and M. M. Krasnow (2018). Form and function in human song. *Current Biology, 28*(3), 356–368.

Mesagno, C., D. Marchant, and T. Morris (2009). Alleviating choking: The sounds of distraction. *Journal of Applied Sport Psychology, 21*(2), 131–147.

Miller, G. (2000). Evolution of human music through sexual selection. In *The Origins of Music*, edited by N. L. Wallin, B. Merker, and S. Brown. Cambridge: The MIT Press, 329–360.

Miluk-Kolasa, B., Z. Obminski, R. Stupnicki, and L. Golec (1994). Effects of music treatment on salivary cortisol in patients exposed to pre-surgical stress. *Experimental and Clinical Endocrinology & Diabetes, 102*(02), 118–120.

Mogul: The Life and Death of Chris Lighty. Parts 1–6, Gimlet Media, Air Dates: June–July 2017. https://www.gimlet media.com/mogul/all#all-episodes-list

Monahan, J. L., S. T. Murphy, and R. B. Zajonc (2000). Subliminal mere exposure: Specific, general, and diffuse effects. *Psychological Science, 11*(6), 462–466.

Moore, M. T., and D. M. Fresco (2012). Depressive realism: A meta-analytic review. *Clinical Psychology Review, 32*(6), 496–509.

Mosing, M. A., G. Madison, N. L. Pedersen, R. Kuja-Halkola, and F. Ullén (2014). Practice does not make perfect: No causal effect of music practice on music ability. *Psychological Science, 25*(9), 1795–1803.

Münte, T. F., E. Altenmüller, and L. Jäncke (2002). The musician's brain as a model of neuroplasticity. *Nature Reviews Neuroscience, 3*(6), 473.

Nantais, K. M., and E. G. Schellenberg (1999). The Mozart effect: An artifact of preference. *Psychological Science, 10*(4), 370–373.

Nilsson, U. (2009). Soothing music can increase oxytocin levels during bed rest after open-heart surgery: A randomised control trial. *Journal of Clinical Nursing, 18*(15), 2153–2161.

North, A. C., and D. J. Hargreaves (1999). Music and adolescent identity. *Music Education Research, 1*(1), 75–92.

Norton, A., L. Zipse, S. Marchina, and G. Schlaug (2009). Melodic intonation therapy. *Annals of the New York Academy of Sciences, 1169*(1), 431–436.

Orr, M. G., and S. Ohlsson (2005). Relationship between complexity and liking as a function of expertise. *Music Perception: An Interdisciplinary Journal, 22*(4), 583–611.

Overy, K., and I. Molnar-Szakacs (2009). Being together in time: Musical experience and the mirror neuron system. *Music Perception: An Interdisciplinary Journal, 26*(5), 489–504.

Pacchetti, C., F. Mancini, R. Aglieri, C. Fundarò, E. Martignoni, and G. Nappi (2000). Active music therapy in Parkinson's disease: An integrative method for motor and emotional rehabilitation. *Psychosomatic Medicine, 62*(3), 386–393.

Panksepp, J. (1995). The emotional sources of "chills" induced by music. *Music Perception: An Interdisciplinary Journal, 13*(2), 171–207.

Panksepp, J., and G. Bernatzky (2002). Emotional sounds and the brain: The neuro-affective foundations of musical appreciation. *Behavioural Processes, 60*(2), 133–155.

Patel, A. D. (2010). *Music, language, and the brain.* Oxford: Oxford University Press.

Pereira, C. S., J. Teixeira, P. Figueiredo, J. Xavier, S. L. Castro, and E. Brattico (2011). Music and emotions in the brain: Familiarity matters. *PLoS ONE, 6*(11), e27241.

Peretz, I. (2013). The biological foundations of music: Insights from congenital amusia. In *The Psychology of Music (Third Edition)*, edited by D. Deutsch. Waltham, MA: Academic Press, 551–564.

Persico, G., L. Antolini, P. Vergani, W. Costantini, M. T. Nardi, and L. Bellotti (2017). Maternal singing of lullabies during pregnancy and after birth: Effects on mother-infant bonding and on newborns' behavior: Concurrent cohort study. *Women and Birth, 30*(4), 214–220.

Pinker, S. (1997). *How the Mind Works.* New York: Norton.

Rabinowitch, T. C., I. Cross, and P. Burnard (2013). Long-term musical group interaction has a positive influence on empathy in children. *Psychology of Music, 41*(4), 484–498.

Rauscher, F., D. Robinson, and J. Jens. (1998). Improved maze learning through early music exposure in rats. *Neurological Research, 20*(5), 427–432.

Rauscher, F. H., G. L. Shaw, and C. N. Ky (1993). Music and spatial task performance. *Nature, 365*(6447), 611.

Richardson, A. J., J. R. Burton, R. P. Sewell, T. F. Spreckelsen, and P. Montgomery (2012). Docosahexaenoic acid for reading, cognition and behavior in children aged 7–9 years: A randomized, controlled trial (the DOLAB Study). *PLoS ONE, 7*(9), e43909.

Rolston, B. (2001). "This is not a rebel song": The Irish conflict and popular music. *Race & Class, 42*(3), 49–67.

Salimpoor, V. N., M. Benovoy, K. Larcher, A. Dagher, and R. J. Zatorre (2011). Anatomically distinct dopamine release during anticipation and experience of peak emotion to music. *Nature Neuroscience, 14*(2), 257.

Salimpoor, V. N., M. Benovoy, G. Longo, J. R. Cooperstock, and R. J. Zatorre (2009). The rewarding aspects of music listening are related to degree of emotional arousal. *PLoS ONE, 4*(10), e7487.

Salimpoor, V. N., I. van den Bosch, N. Kovacevic, A. R. McIntosh, A. Dagher, and R. J. Zatorre (2013). Interactions between the nucleus accumbens and auditory cortices predict music reward value. *Science, 340*(6129), 216–219.

Sapolsky, R. On *Radiolab*: Revising the Fault Line. Air Date: June 27, 2017. https://www.wnycstudios.org/story/revising-fault-line/

Schellenberg, E. G. (2004). Music lessons enhance IQ. *Psychological Science, 15*(8), 511–514.

Schellenberg, E. G. (2006). Long-term positive associations between music lessons and IQ. *Journal of Educational Psychology, 98*(2), 457.

Schlaug, G., M. Forgeard, L. Zhu, A. Norton, and E. Winner (2009). Training-induced neuroplasticity in young children. *Annals of the New York Academy of Sciences, 1169*(1), 205–208.

Schlaug, G., L. Jäncke, Y. Huang, J. F. Staiger, and H. Steinmetz (1995). Increased corpus callosum size in musicians. *Neuropsychologia, 33*(8), 1047–1055.

Schlaug, G., S. Marchina, and A. Norton (2009). Evidence for plasticity in white-matter tracts of patients with chronic Broca's aphasia undergoing intense intonation-based speech therapy. *Annals of the New York Academy of Sciences, 1169*(1), 385–394.

Simmons-Stern, N. R., A. E. Budson, and B. A. Ally (2010). Music as a memory enhancer in patients with Alzheimer's disease. *Neuropsychologia, 48*(10), 3164–3167.

Skoe, E., and N. Kraus (2012). A little goes a long way: How the adult brain is shaped by musical training in childhood. *Journal of Neuroscience, 32*(34), 11507–11510.

Snowdon, C. T., and D. Teie (2010). Affective responses in tamarins elicited by species-specific music. *Biology Letters, 6*(1), 30–32.

Snowdon, C. T., and D. Teie (2013). Emotional communication in monkeys: Music to their ears? In *The Evolution of Emotional Communication: From Sounds in Nonhuman Mammals to Speech and Music in Man*, edited by E. Altenmüller, S. Schmidt, and E. Zimmerman. Oxford: Oxford University Press, 133–151.

Soley, G., and E. E. Hannon (2010). Infants prefer the musical meter of their own culture: A cross-cultural comparison. *Developmental Psychology, 46*(1), 286.

Standley, J. M. (2008). Does music instruction help children learn to read? Evidence of a meta-analysis. *Update: Applications of Research in Music Education, 27*(1), 17–32.

Stefano, G. B., W. Zhu, P. Cadet, E. Salamon, and K. J. Mantione (2004). Music alters constitutively expressed opiate and cytokine processes in listeners. *Medical Science Monitor, 10*(6), MS18–MS27.

Steinberg, M. (2000). *The Concerto: A Listener's Guide.* Oxford: Oxford University Press, 485.

Stephens-Davidowitz, S. (2018). The songs that bind. *New York Times.* Retrieved from https://www.nytimes.com/2018/02/10/opinion/sunday/favorite-songs.html

Tarr, B., J. Launay, and R. I. Dunbar (2014). Music and social bonding: "Self-other" merging and neurohormonal mechanisms. *Frontiers in Psychology, 5,* 1096.

Terry, P. C., C. I. Karageorghis, A. M. Saha, and S. D'Auria (2012). Effects of synchronous music on treadmill running among elite triathletes. *Journal of Science and Medicine in Sport, 15*(1), 52–57.

Thompson, W. F., E. G. Schellenberg, and G. Husain (2001). Arousal, mood, and the Mozart effect. *Psychological Science, 12*(3), 248–251.

Trainor, L. J., and B. M. Heinmiller (1998). The development of evaluative responses to music: Infants prefer to listen to consonance over dissonance. *Infant Behavior and Development, 21*(1), 77–88.

Trehub, S. E. (2003). The developmental origins of musicality. *Nature Neuroscience 6*(7): 669–673.

Trehub, S. E. (2003). Musical predispositions in infancy. In *The Cognitive Neuroscience of Music*, edited by I. Peretz and R. J. Zatorre. Oxford: Oxford University Press.

Ullmann, Y., L. Fodor, I. Schwarzberg, N. Carmi, A. Ullmann, and Y. Ramon (2008). The sounds of music in the operating room. *Injury, 39*(5), 592–597.

Van de Winckel, A., H. Feys, W. De Weerdt, and R. Dom (2004). Cognitive and behavioural effects of music-based exercises in patients with dementia. *Clinical Rehabilitation, 18*(3), 253–260.

Van Praag, H., T. Shubert, C. Zhao, and F. H. Gage (2005). Exercise enhances learning and hippocampal neurogenesis in aged mice. *Journal of Neuroscience, 25*(38), 8680–8685.

Vuust, P., and C. D. Frith (2008) Anticipation is the key to understanding music and the effects of music on emotion. *Behavioral and Brain Sciences, 31*: 599–600.

Wallace, W. T. (1994). Memory for music: Effect of melody on recall of text. *Journal of Experimental Psychology: Learning, Memory, and Cognition, 20*(6), 1471.

Wang, S. M., L. Kulkarni, J. Dolev, and Z. N. Kain (2002). Music and preoperative anxiety: A randomized, controlled study. *Anesthesia & Analgesia, 94*(6), 1489–1494.

White-Schwoch, T., K. W. Carr, S. Anderson, D. L. Strait, and N. Kraus (2013). Older adults benefit from music training early in life: Biological evidence for long-term training-driven plasticity. *Journal of Neuroscience, 33*(45), 17667–17674.

Williamson, V. J., S. R. Jilka, J. Fry, S. Finkel, D. Müllensiefen, and L. Stewart (2012). How do "earworms" start? Classifying the everyday circumstances of involuntary musical imagery. *Psychology of Music, 40*(3), 259–284.

Williamson, V. J., L. A. Liikkanen, K. Jakubowski, and L. Stewart (2014). Sticky tunes: How do people react to involuntary musical imagery? *PLoS ONE, 9*(1), e86170.

Wittmann, M., and S. Lehnhoff (2005). Age effects in perception of time. *Psychological Reports, 97*(3), 921–935.

Zajonc, R. B. (2001). Mere exposure: A gateway to the subliminal. *Current Directions in Psychological Science, 10*(6), 224–228.

ACKNOWLEDGMENTS

Thank you to my editor, Mirabelle Korn, for making this book immeasurably better while keeping my ego fully intact. Thank you also to Christina Amini, whose vision for the project brought the book to life. Thank you to the crew at Chronicle, including Vanessa Dina, Maggie Edelman, Janine Sato, Meghan Legg, and Michele Posner. I'm also deeply grateful to Anne Germanacos, whose support of my work over the years has given me the freedom to develop my ideas in unconventional ways. Thank you also to Adam Isaak, who edits and produces my podcast *Cadence: What music tells us about the mind*, which served as the foundation for this project. Thanks to Matching Half Café where most of the writing took place, fueled by coffee and bagels. I'm also grateful to my music teachers, especially Jane Randolph, Marjorie Sparks, and Kristin Pankonin, who believed I was worth the investment of their time and made me a better musician.

Thanks to my psychology mentors, especially Morris Moscovitch, Mary Pat McAndrews, and Barbara Knowlton, who encouraged me to find my own path at the intersection of science and art. I'm also indebted to Rita and Jonathan Lynn for their unwavering support and insightful advice. Thank you Adam and AJ, for giving me the space to think and for filling my days with joy and laughter. Finally, I'd like to thank my mother, who taught me from the very beginning that music makes everything better.